Hiding Out

For Peter and Luke

Also by Irene Rawnsley

**Ask a Silly Question
Dog's Dinner
The House of a Hundred Cats**

Acknowledgements

HIDING OUT was originally broadcast as a half hour programme in the English Resources series, BBC Schools Radio. Since then several of the poems have appeared singly in text books and anthologies.

'Down at the Launderette' was published in the GCSE O-level English anthology 1994-95, by the Northern Examinations and Assessment Board.

'Pets' was first published in *The House of a Hundred Cats* (Methuen Children's Books, 1995)

Irene Rawnsley

Hiding Out

Smith/Doorstop Books

Published 1996 by
Smith/Doorstop Books
The Poetry Business
The Studio
Byram Arcade
Westgate
Huddersfield HD1 1ND

Copyright © Irene Rawnsley 1996

ISBN 1 869961 56 0

A CIP catalogue record for this title is available from the British Library

Printed by Swiftprint, Huddersfield

The Poetry Business gratefully acknowledges the help of the Arts Council of England, Kirklees Metropolitan Council and Yorkshire & Humberside Arts.

This book is sold subject to the condition that it shall not, by way of trade or otherwise, be lent, resold, hired out, or otherwise circulated without the publisher's prior consent in any form of binding or cover other than that in which it is published and without a similar condition being imposed on the subsequent purchaser.

Contents

Friends and Enemies
Pedal Pushing	9
Graffiti	10
The Belly Fund	11
One Morning	12
Vital Statistics	13
The Caretaker's Poems	14
Money	15
Dracula's Daughter	16

Jason
Mastermind	18
Pets	20
Not Guilty	21
Moody Glue	22
Down At The Launderette	24
Assembly	25

Sandy
Conversation	28
Sandy's Letter To Santa Claus	29
Sandy's Letter	30
Absent	32

Stevo
Local Industry	34
Lies	35
Pal	36
Stealing	38

Jesmond Street
Changes	40
Staying On	41
Lost	42
17 Jesmond Street	44
Stevo's Bedtime Story	46
Ghosts?	47
Hiding Out	48
Neighbours	49
Dead End	50

Police and Parents
Cover Up	52
Waiting	54
Pete The Feet Visits School	55

Friends and Enemies

Pedal Pushing

The promise of good times
was in the air; cemetery trees
dropped gold leaves on graves
in sunshine reminding the dead

of all they were missing
when who should bicycle
to the usual meeting place
but James Bell, no-one's mate,

huge knees rising, falling
rhythmically, flares flapping.
'Who asked you to come?'
'Meself.' He pushed his machine

towards them, a makeshift bike
of strangely matched components
with stuffed plastic saddle.
'Wherever did you get this?'

'Built it. When I heard about
you lot riding to Dewsbury
I collected parts on the tip.
Finished it yesterday.'

Made mute the group put feet
on pedals, set wheels in motion,
moved off, Big Belly following;
nobody tried to stop him.

Graffiti

Sprayed on the wall
of the underpass
VOTE FOR BELLY
no kid would dare
do otherwise.

Always
in every situation
Big Bell gets his way.

The Belly Fund

Alone Big Belly
waits for
his customers

knows they'll come
to part reluctantly
with ten pence

twenty, fifty
whatever they've
managed to save

or steal securing
another few days
fear free.

Thick fingers
post coins into
his overcoat

'I call it
my pocket money'
enter names

in the notebook
which one day
will page his guilt.

One Morning

A lunatic bicycle decorates
the school gymnasium roof;
policeman helps caretaker
lift it down. They examine it.
Painted red, stickers everywhere,
cow-horn handlebars upside down,
stuffed plastic bag for saddle.
'Toss you for which of us rides it
to the Station,' says Pete Police.
He wins; it makes his day.

Vital Statistics

He used chest expanders
in the early years to reach
the forty two that
fills his tunic jacket.

Now, at six foot three
without the helmet
he's impressive,
a force to be reckoned with.

Blue suits him;
his uniform walks tall.
Nobody laughs any more
at his size twelve boots.

The Caretaker's Poems

Roses are red,
Violets are blue.
Bubble gum's pink;
It sticks like glue
to the corners

of the stacking tables
in the dining room.
Sometimes I have
a hell of a job
unstacking them.

***

Christmas comes but once a year,
Of that I am convinced;
I'd give a lot for a nice new school
Without no fingerprints.

No gruesome carvings on the desks,
No rude words on the wall,
No paint spilled on the parky floor,
No mud across the hall.

No kids to kick footballs on the roof,
Or stuff things down the loo,
And now I come to think of it
I'd have no teachers too.

Money

'is the root of all evil,'
warns Mr.Hardaker,
giving his annual
economics lesson.

He dresses like he has none;
carries a string-handled
veteran briefcase
into which he stuffs

each day's marking,
a sandwich box,
the Financial Times to read
on his bus journey home.

'You'll learn this doesn't
grow on trees;' waves
his wallet in front of them,
a visual aid.

'Where do you work, Sir?'
jokes Stevo. The teacher
tucks his money safe
inside his jacket and smiles.

Dracula's Daughter

She climbs out of her coffin
every morning, puts on
an old fur coat and drives
to school to be a teacher.

During the day she seems
almost human, though a shade
too interested in
the history of tombstones.

Giveaways are long black hair,
fondness for red ink,
the silver bat she sometimes
pins to her lapel.

Pupils are wary of her smile,
having glimpsed
through staffroom curtains
her ritual nail-sharpening;

Always they watch her moods
fearing how thin she is;
someone heard her say
she likes young blood about her.

Jason

Mastermind

Your chosen subject is
Mr. Hardaker, starting now;
what's his favourite lesson?

Geography. He's always going on
about places he's been,
India, the Isle of Man, Skegness.

Tell me his nickname.

Hardy. Another teacher called
Laurel left last term.

How old is he?

About ninety.

Has he any hobbies?

He is passionately in love
with Miss Dracula.
She likes him as well.

How do you know?

She laughs at his unfunny jokes.

Will they get married?

He's too mean. When the
Lifeboat box came round
I saw him putting in ten pence.

Where does he live?

Set that one for homework; you're
beginning to sound like him yourself.

Pets

When I was in the Infants I pinched
the school's goldfish. I felt sorry for them,
one tiny meal a day, not much water,
swimming in circles watching us do sums;
I decided to free them in the canal.

My mate Mitch hid with me after school
in the cloakroom, pretending to be
looking for a coat when the cleaner came;
after she'd gone we raided our classroom
for the bowl. The canal was a long way;

We were walking really slow, trying not
to slop the water when we met Mrs. Sparks
the school secretary who demanded to know
where we were going. 'Taking these fish home.
An old man was giving them away as pets.'

But she recognized the bowl, ordered us
to carry them back. Afterwards they bought
a proper aquarium to keep the fish healthy
so we rescued the guinea pig. He had
a great time with us before they found out.

Not Guilty

My left boot
keeps kicking people.
When they walk by
it seems to try tripping
them up; I'm always
getting done for it.

My mouth spits paper.
Like cowboys I chew it
then shoot; television
taught me to do it
but Sir blames me
when kids complain.

Excuses come easy
as cartoon bubbles
when I'm in trouble;
what else can I do if
my tongue invents things
that aren't true?

Moody Glue

'Listen, kid,
Come with me tonight,
Don't run away
I won't start a fight
I'm showing you
The moody glue.

Now then, kid,
Hold your head on tight,
It'll be so good
If you do it right;
It's something new,
The moody glue.'

Back home I locked
My bedroom door;
'It's homework, dad,
What d'you want me for?'
That wasn't true;
It was moody glue.

I tried to find
That boy next day;
His mates said
'Sniffer's gone away.'
They all knew
About his moody glue.

'You'll never see
Your friend again;
He was taken away
By ambulance men
All cold and blue
From his moody glue.'

I keep my secret
Safe inside;
It could have been me
That night who died;
I guess I'm through
With the moody glue.

Down At The Launderette

First time I ran away I was only eight.
St. Stephens and Redgates had planned
a fight; I tagged along with the fourth years
marching in a gang, everyone dead hard
but the fight was off, the police came;
I didn't want to leave before the action
so I hung around to see what would happen.

It grew cold after dark; I shivered
with my hands stuck up the sleeves
of my jersey, too scared to go home.
The gang said they knew where to get warm,
took me to the launderette where
a woman had unloaded her tumble drier.
'Climb in there quick; it's still hot.'

Then they shut the door, put money in,
just for the laugh. The attendant had
a key to unlock me but she threatened
to call the police if we didn't leave
so we moved off, me with grazed knees,
limping, laughing; they were saying
'He's a hard case, this kid, dead hard.'

Assembly

What do they think we are,
robots? Bits and pieces
kept behind classroom doors
in tidy boxes

to be put together
every Monday morning,
programmed for the week
to say 'Yes Sir

'No Sir' line up
sit down, speak
when you're spoken to
always wear school uniform?

Robots don't give hassle,
don't swear, smoke, fight,
tell lies, steal,
or play tricks on the staff.

Teachers think they'd like that
but who would laugh
at their jokes?
Robots have no sense of humour.

If you asked any robot
why the chicken
crossed the road
he'd be stuck for an answer.

They don't smile or talk much,
only think what they've
been taught to think.
Dead boring, being a robot.

Sandy

Conversation

You never told me,
why did the chicken
cross the road?

He wanted to watch the match.

I didn't know
chickens liked football.

This one did. He was
thrown out of the
Laygold factory
for producing round eggs.

What did he do?

Became a tramp.
Slept in bus shelters,
crossed roads until
his accident.

What happened,
was he run over?

No, he was trampled
underfoot by a zebra
coming the other way.

Sandy's Letter To Santa Claus

I know you don't exist
but just in case
you're making up the list
for next year

I want a sports bag
with a zip and handles;
kids all laugh
at my big satchel.

I've got enough atlases
and encyclopaedias,
I'd rather have books
about animals,

and I'd like a bike,
a Mountain Muddy Fox
if that's possible,
but if you can't bring

any of these I'd
choose a Siamese cat;
its food would be
my responsibility.

Sandy's Letter

S is for Sandy,
slow at doing things,
someone who doesn't
like arguing,
that's me.

At school Sir says
I'm a scatterbrain;
'Forget your head
if it was loose'
he says.

Forgot my homework.
Now there's a letter
sitting in my school bag
telling my parents,
'Sandy must improve.'

I'd like to screw it up,
shred it, see the bits
sail away like birds
but Sir says he'll phone
for an answer.

I'll not go home.
If I do they'll only
scream and shout at me
and at each other;
I'm sick of it.

After dark I'll
slip a note through
the letterbox
saying I've gone.
From now on Sandy's
living on his own.

Absent

Missing the register's
best about being away;
'Alexander Smith' he'll call,
'Speak up Alexander,
we can't hear you

Alexander' he always says
to make them laugh;
he knows I'm called Sandy
'Alexander' but I won't
be in my place with

Big Belly's ruler
boring into my back
'Speak up, Alexander'
'Away Sir' they'll all say,
'Sandy Smith's away'

Stevo

Local Industry

Rhubarb once grew where
the pop works stands
my dad used to play
hiddy between stems
high as houses dip
little stalks in sugar

To eat on his way to
school we have to walk
the long way round
a fence keeps you out
except if the watchman's
at the other side

We sneak under the wire
to pinch empty bottles
from the crates you can
get money sometimes if
you take them back
to the right shops

Lies

My father lied for me
when I refused to go to school
no special reason
except it was Monday
and raining
I blamed a headache but
he knew it wasn't true

He brought me aspirins
in a glass of water
said 'your mother would
have known what to do'
then I heard him phone
'there's been a spot of
trouble in the past

I'd like to let you know
today he's genuinely ill'
teatime he asked me
'how are you now son?'
my head was thumping from
watching videos all day
'fine' I said 'just fine'

Pal

My mam bought me a palomino
he was ace that horse
bigger than the police horses
you see at Leeds United
I stabled him at Moor's where
I used to work Saturdays
mucking out

She bought me a leather saddle
with all the tackle
I used to leap on his back
trot around the field
but Pal always wanted
to gallop he didn't like
going slow

Night times he was best
when they were all in bed
I'd sneak across the field
to the stable and call 'Pal'
he'd breathe into my hand
with his nose like he
was kissing me

And we would gallop miles
we leapt a river once he
was so strong his hooves
just splashed the water
jumped hedges so high we

didn't come down for ages
like flying

My mam bought me a palomino
once from Blackpool or
perhaps it was for Christmas
I can't remember which
he died my palomino or
maybe my dad sold him but
I'm missing him

Stealing

He came downstairs
shouting 'where's my money?'
dressed in the jacket

that he always wears
for the pub I guessed
he'd been looking

under the clothes in
the chest of drawers
he keeps a spare wallet

for a rainy day I only
took a note now
and again thinking he

wouldn't notice 'where's
my money?' I didn't
wait to get hit

Jesmond Street

Changes

Snotty Joe at the chippy
remembers prosperous times
on Jesmond Street

when brisk brown fish lay
three layers deep above
the silver pans

and he was never short
of newspapers to wrap them.
Now children queue

out of the cold for
bags of chips with scraps,
amuse their waiting

by writing on the steamy walls
and windows. Joe watches
without complaint,

reads his own fortune in
the messages breeding
layer on greasy layer.

Staying On

Left behind by the van
which took away everything
familiar to him,

hearthrug, cushions, dish,
table scratching post, the cat
decided to stay on

but found life sharply
changed. He who had
never been much of a hunter

now flattened his belly,
crouched by holes, learned
finer skills of scent and hearing,

became animal cautious.
He could not bring himself to cringe
on strangers' doorsteps

so he came and went
through his own home cellar grating;
slept in the cold, drank

from drips and rain pools.
He took with dignity the new
harshness, lived without friends,

his only enemy the cough
which rattled his chest
and would not leave him be.

Lost

'This is the key
that opens the door
of the house on the street
where I live.

These are the shoes
that walked to the shop
but won't take me back
to the house on the street
where I live.

This is the pension
in my purse
inside the bag
that goes with the shoes
that won't walk back
to the house on the street
where I live.'

Here's the policeman
tall and kind
knows Mrs.Edgerton's
uncertain mind;

Carries her bag
and takes her arm,
leads her home
to the house on the street
where she lives.

Here's the report
that he makes at the station;
'Area due for demolition
but she won't move.
She's the last one left
in a house on the street
where she lives.'

17 Jesmond Street

Social Worker Sue walks
the path avoiding cracks like
a little girl who still believes
in magic. She will need

something of the sort; Janey
hates official visitors. To ring
the doorbell is seldom any use;
she calls through the letterbox.

'See what I've brought you!'
Toffees tumble from the slot to
join a litter of neglected post;
Janey hears but chooses not to.

'Someone been upsetting you again?
It's only Sue; we'll talk.'
Looking through the slit
she sees the old lady enter

the kitchen. 'Making tea, love?
I'd like some.' Half a lie, this;
drinking from cracked china
on a damp chair in a house

smelling of rot has hardly
been pleasant. 'Open up, dear
I have something urgent to say.'
This is true but Janey ignores

her visitor and noisily fills
the kettle. She turns a gas tap
full on then looks for matches.
'Dearie, I must talk to you.'

After the explosion Janey drops
the spent match, unlocks the door.
'I came to tell you, love;
they're cutting off your gas today.'

Stevo's Bedtime Story

Once upon a time
there were three little pigs
who ran away to live
in an old house where
there was only them

They were hungry
these pigs so they nicked
sweets from supermarkets
and milk from people's steps
but the wolf never caught them

The first little pig
found loads of money stuffed
in an armchair he went
to Scotland to see his mam
and he was happy

The second pig
made it to London he was
the youngest player
ever fielded by Arsenal
and he was happy

The third pig was miserable
for his mam and dad but
he was scared to go back
he cried 'wee wee wee'
all the way home

Ghosts?

Of course there's ghosts; old houses
are full of them; folk don't disappear
completely after they move away;
traces of them remain

trapped inside forever, waiting
night time chances to come alive.
It only needs the wind to wake,
soot to settle, a few dust curls

to slip across an empty floor;
there'll be the scratch of pens
on football coupons; knitting needles,
dominoes clicking, everything

they liked to do before they moved away.
Listen for ghosts tonight; you'll catch
faint happenings in darkness;
hold your breath, you'll hear them.

Hiding Out

Thumped almost unconscious
by his own heartbeat
a boy shelters in the dark,
hiding out in this house,
a runaway's refuge.

With candles snuffed
into the reek of rotten timber
old darknesses crowd the room,
press upon him, holding
him prisoner. The house

wraps him in his own skin
like a parcel posted
to the wrong address, thrown
aside until morning. Captive
he folds his hands

over his eyes fearing
the stain of blackness;
keeps his mouth shut tight,
tries not to hear
the scuffles that might be
rats scurrying near.

Neighbours

The house cries at night sometimes,
from loneliness; I hear brick bones creak,
it never expected to be left alone.
There was Mrs.Hook, she's gone. 'Janey,'
she would say, 'Take care of that heart'
but it was her the ambulance took away.

Have another biscuit, they're not soft;
I bought them from the shop myself
yesterday and put them straight in a tin;
we're careful of the damp in these houses
but I'm fine with the gas fire, I sleep
in the chair; night time, day, I don't care.

Men from the council, they're always trying
to shift me; watch out, they'll be after you
if you stay next door. Old folk, young,
nobody bothers any more. I was twelve
when I started work, did well at sewing,
a machine by fifteen, not many can claim that.

Knock if there's anything you need.
Bessie Hook used to say nobody could hope
for a better neighbour, though she was nosey.
She'd want to know why you're sleeping out
in an empty house without parents. Not me,
no questions asked. Have another biscuit.

Dead End

And the garden said, 'Let there be
an end to cauliflowers, cabbages,
curly kale and cucumbers.
May beans not run,
turnips turn on blanching celery,
carrots beet broccoli.

Let there be no more cane-cutting,
cornering, notching, nicking,
pricking out, potting up, digging in,
damping down, drenching,
grafting, grubbing, binding, banding,
ringing or dead-heading.

May rust confuse the arms of clippers
that would trim, tame and tamper;
let them lie undisturbed with
forks, rakes, riddles, edgers,
hoes, trowels, all that would trouble
the mouldering earth.

Let there be blight and mildew;
bitter pit, black leg, bud blast.
May mice invade; slugworms, wireworms,
leather jackets, woodlice, woolly aphids,
weevils, may they scab, scald,
scorch, scale, spit, spot and rot.'

And the garden was not.

Police and Parents

Cover Up

Police at the door again;
usual questions, vandalism, kids
messing about on the railway line
and where has my son been?

'He's been asleep since nine,'
I told them but he hasn't.
When I came home from work at six
his tea hadn't been touched;

(I always leave a snack between
two plates; my mother used
to do the same for me)
he'd taken his new trainers,

small change from the milk money
and gone, God knows where,
s ome place like last time I expect;
he'll be back when he's hungry.

I had hoped the Social Worker
would have talked sense
into him at his interviews,
persuaded him to avoid trouble,

but no, it's all happening again,
lies, school phoning me at work
to ask where is he, no-good louts
waiting for him in the street.

If I stop his money he steals,
hit him, he runs. You can't
keep your own son prisoner
for ever; I've given up trying.

I've been father and mother to him,
fed, clothed him, done my best;
nobody can say otherwise. Some kids
will turn out bad whatever you do.

Waiting

No news isn't good news;
No news nags like toothache
Through six o'clock, seven
When Sandy's not home from school.

No news searches the streets,
Park, supermarket, places where
He could and couldn't be;
Asks everyone.

No news imagines him kidnapped,
Drowned in the canal,
Sleeping rough, beaten up,
Crying to come home.

No news can't eat or think,
Hears twenty times the gate
Click, sees a school bag
Swinging on the kitchen hook.

No news won't go to bed,
Watches the telephone, longs
To spite its silence with
A boy come back tonight.

Pete The Feet Visits School

I found them making afternoon tea
in the gardens behind Jesmond Street,
those empty houses to be pulled down.
They had it all organized, fire,
kettle boiling, cups, a couple
of old armchairs to sit in,
home from home.

The little ginger one gave me
a run for my money; I tripped but
caught him with a rugby tackle.
Smith, he's called, not been in trouble
before but he soon will be again
if he hangs around with those two.
Cried when I took him back.

I've cautioned each of them;
entering unoccupied property,
breaking a window, theft of milk.
Makes you wonder what goes on
in their heads, these kids,
how far did they think they'd get,
no money, on their own?

I've talked to the parents.
The Smiths were out of their minds
with worry but Lambert's father
seemed engrossed in his own problems.
Needs to think about his boy before

it's too late. Fletcher's dad has
given him another good belting.

They'll be brought to school Monday.
Please inform us if they don't arrive,
they've been warned about truanting;
mustn't let them get away with it.
Explain how worried everyone's been.
Tell them we all have days when
we feel like running away.